WHAT we ♥LOVE most about LIFE ♥

Answers from 150 children across the autism spectrum

COMPILED BY
CHRIS BONNELLO
OF AUTISTICNOTWEIRD.COM

DESIGNED BY NANCY J. PRICE OF MYRIA.COM

What We Love Most About Life:
Answers from 150 Children Across the Autism Spectrum

Formatting note: As this book project originated in the United Kingdom,
British spelling, grammar and punctuation is used throughout.

Cover design & book design © by Nancy J Price | Synchronista.com | USA

First Edition | First Printing | Printed in England

http://AutisticNotWeird.com

Foreword

"I have autism. And you know what? I love it."

It took me until the age of 30 to say those words. I was giving a talk to a group of parents who had children on the autism spectrum, plenty of whom were worried for their kids' futures. I could have told them I'd just learned to cope with being autistic, but I didn't think that would be enough. I want to be positive about autism, instead of just 'not negative'.

In my young adult years, I was affected by depression and anxiety, and one of my coping strategies was to make a list of all the little things I loved about life. My answers ranged from "campfires" to "that feeling just before you see a friend for the first time in ages", and from "colours (seriously, just stop and look at them)" to "having teeth". Having this physical list helped me remember that even when my own life was on unstable ground, life itself was still a wonderful thing.

After Autistic Not Weird took off, I realised that a large anthology of beautiful things – contributed by autistic youngsters worldwide – would be both achievable and beautiful. And, given the negativity that still gets thrown at autism, it was about time we showed how positive we can be when we get to speak for ourselves.

So here it is. A hundred and fifty young people all across the autism spectrum, here in this book to tell you what they love most about life. I hope you find plenty in this book to love, too.

Chris Bonnello

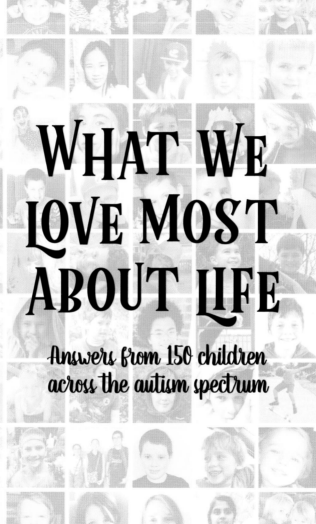

WHAT WE LOVE MOST ABOUT LIFE

Answers from 150 children
across the autism spectrum

Matthew

"THAT I GET TO LIVE IT."

MATTHEW, AGE 12, FROM NORTHAMPTON, ENGLAND
DIAGNOSIS: ASPERGER SYNDROME

"RUNNING, SKIPPING, JUMPING, EXERCISING, LEARNING, ABC'S, MATH, AND MAKING FRIENDS, THAT'S WHAT I LOVE ABOUT LIFE, MOMMY!"

SOFIA, AGE 6, FROM FORT LEWIS, WASHINGTON, USA
DIAGNOSIS: AUTISM

Sofia

Victor

"MY DOGS. ESPECIALLY BELLA. SHE KNOWS HOW I FEEL. I LOVE MY COMPUTER AND IPAD. I LOOK A LOT AT YOUTUBE . I WILL BE A YOUTUBER WHEN I GROW UP. I HAVE JUST STARTED AT A NEW SCHOOL. IT IS FOR AUTISTIC CHILDREN LIKE ME, AND I JUST LOVE IT."

VICTOR, AGE 12, FROM BRØNDERSLEV, NORTH JUTLAND, DENMARK
DIAGNOSIS: AUTISM, ADD

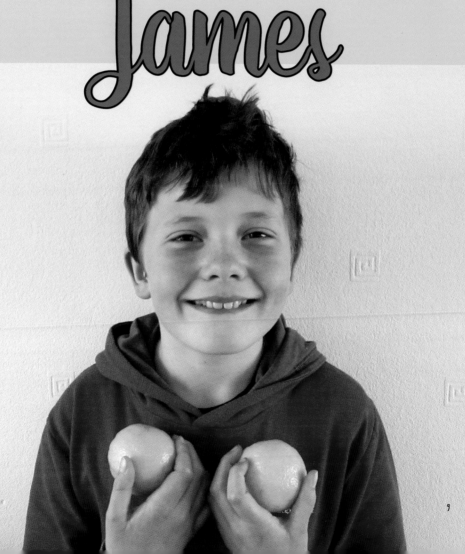

"I LOVE LEMONS BECAUSE
I LIKE HOW SOUR THEY ARE.
THEY TASTE LIKE ELEPHANTS."

JAMES, AGE 11, FROM SOUTHPORT, MERSEYSIDE, ENGLAND
DIAGNOSIS: HF-ASD

James

"WHEN I SPEAK IN A FUNNY VOICE,
IT MAKES ADDY LAUGH.
ADDY IS MY BEST FRIEND. SQUEEZE ME, ADDY!"
(TRANSLATION: SQUEEZE MEANS CHASE.)

ISSY, AGE 4, FROM QUEENSLAND, AUSTRALIA

Issy

Lewis

"OOOH, MOVIES I THINK."

LEWIS, AGE 13, FROM SCOTTISH BORDERS, SCOTLAND
DIAGNOSIS: AUTISM, SEVERE LEARNING DIFFICULTIES

Nathaniel

"THERE'S TOO MANY THINGS TO CHOOSE. I LOVE RIDING MY SCOOTER, PLAYING WITH MY TOYS, MUMMY, AND GOING ON ADVENTURES."

NATHANIEL, AGE 8, FROM HERTFORDSHIRE, ENGLAND – DIAGNOSIS: AUTISM

"NATHANIEL BELIEVES AUTISM GIVES HIM SUPERPOWERS: THE POWERS TO SEE, HEAR AND SMELL THINGS OTHER PEOPLE CAN'T. SOME DAYS IT MAKES HIS HEAD VIBRATE AND TINGLE, BUT IT'S ALL WORTH IT FOR THE SUPERPOWERS! HE SAYS IT'S GOOD TO BE DIFFERENT, BECAUSE BEING THE SAME IS BORING."

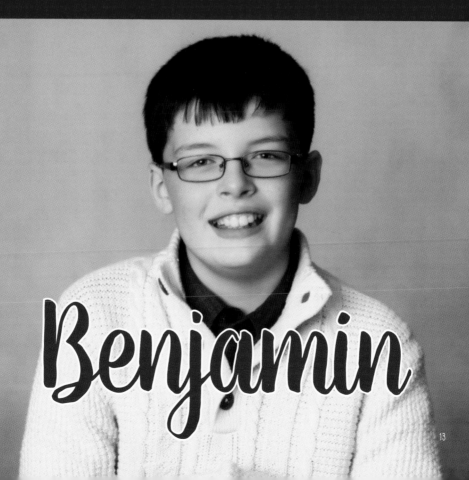

"WHAT I LOVE ABOUT LIFE IS HOW PEOPLE CAN DREAM AND BE WHATEVER THEY WANT TO BE. YOU CAN LET YOUR DREAMS GUIDE YOU AND WORK TOWARDS MAKING THEM A REALITY. NO MATTER HOW ODD, OR DIFFERENT YOU ARE, ONLY YOU DECIDE YOUR FUTURE."

BENJAMIN, AGE 11, FROM PLATTSBURGH, NEW YORK, USA
BENJAMIN RUNS HIS OWN FACEBOOK PAGE, "BENJAMIN GIROUX".
(PHOTO CREDIT: BELTRAMI & CO.)

Benjamin

Joseph

"JOSEPH LOVES BEING OUTSIDE, ANIMALS, BOOKS, TICKLES, AND JOKING AROUND. JOSEPH IS CURRENTLY NON-VERBAL, BUT HIS LAUGH WOULD BRIGHTEN YOUR DARKEST DAY."

JOSEPH, AGE 3, FROM COUNTY CORK, IRELAND

DIAGNOSIS: ASD

"I LOVE THAT I GET TO ENJOY MY FAVOURITE THINGS, LIKE PLAYING PIANO AND BIG HUGS FROM MOMMY, OH AND PLAYING WITH MY SISTERS AND PIZZA."

MYKAH, AGE 8, FROM SEATTLE, WASHINGTON, USA

Mykah

Aiden

"I THOUGHT LEGO WAS THE BEST THING ABOUT LIFE UNTIL I SAW THIS LEGO T.A.R.D.I.S."

AIDEN, AGE 8, FROM NEW SOUTH WALES, AUSTRALIA

DIAGNOSIS: ASD, ADHD, ODD, ANXIETY (HIS BROTHER NICHOLAS IS ON THE OPPOSITE PAGE)

"I THINK THE BEST THING ABOUT LIFE IS I CAN BE CAPTAIN AUSTRALIA WHEN I GROW UP."

NICHOLAS, AGE 6, FROM NEW SOUTH WALES, AUSTRALIA
DIAGNOSIS: ASD, HYPERMOBILITY (BROTHER OF AIDEN ON OPPOSITE PAGE)

Nicholas

Joshua

"I LOVE MY FAMILY, MY DOG PEPPER, MY XBOX AND MY TOY, SADNESS, WHO MAKES ME FEEL SAFE. CHEESE!"

JOSHUA, AGE 11, FROM WORCESTER, ENGLAND – DIAGNOSIS: AUTISM, PDA

Connor + Aiden

BROTHERS FROM BIRMINGHAM, ENGLAND

CONNOR AGREED TO BE IN THE BOOK ON THE CONDITION THAT HE COULD TELL ME THIS JOKE: CONNOR: "CHRIS, LOOK UNDER THERE." ME: "UNDER WHERE?" CONNOR: "MADE YOU SAY UNDERWEAR!"

CONNOR AND AIDEN'S FATHER RUNS A FACEBOOK PAGE CALLED "AUTISM: FROM A DAD'S EYE VIEW"

"THE THINGS I LOVE ABOUT LIFE ARE MY FAMILY, MY MOMMY, MY FRIENDS... I LIKE ADVENTURES, DRAWING, MY JOKES."

CONNOR, AGE 9 – DIAGNOSIS: HIGH FUNCTIONING ASD, ADD, ADHD

"AIDEN LOVES SEEKING OUT ALL THE SENSES IN THE WORLD. HE LOVES TO SEE AND FEEL EVERYTHING. HE SEARCHES OUT PHYSICAL STIMULUS AND WILL LAUGH WHEN HE IS HAVING FUN. HE IS A VERY LOVING BOY, AND WILL SHOW IT IN MANY DIFFERENT WAYS."

AIDEN, AGE 7 – SEVERE AUTISM (NON-VERBAL), HYPOSENSITIVE SENSORY SEEKER

Annabelle

"I'M GOING TO SAY PLAYING, 'CAUSE WHEN ALL THE KIDS PLAY, KIDS ALL SAME, NO KID IS NOT SAME. AND DYE MY HAIR 'CAUSE OF THE COLOURS, I LIKE THE COLOURS, 'CAUSE NO ONE ELSE HAS MY COLOURS, AND THEN I'M DIFFERENT 'CAUSE I MADE IT DIFFERENT, AND IT PRETTY."

ANNABELLE, AGE 10, FROM ADELAIDE, SOUTH AUSTRALIA – DIAGNOSIS: AUTISM

"IT'S A FACT YOU HAVE AUTISM, BUT YOU CHOOSE WHAT YOU DO WITH IT. FIND THE PROS IN YOUR PERSONALITY; TRY TO LIVE THROUGH THE CONS. AFTER ALL, LIFE EXISTS TO EXIST, AND THERE'S NO CHANGING WHO YOU ARE. AUTISM? MORE LIKE AWESOME-TISM!"

FINLEY, AGE 11, FROM EAST SUSSEX, ENGLAND
DIAGNOSIS: ASD

Finley

Lucca

"YOUTUBE! AND FAMILY... BUT YOUTUBE FIRST. JUST KIDDING! MUM AND DAD FIRST, BUT YOUTUBE DEFINITELY SECOND! FAMILY IS THE MOST IMPORTANT, BUT I WOULD NOT WANT TO LIVE WITHOUT YOUTUBE, THE INTERNET AND WI-FI."

LUCCA, AGE 12, FROM ASTEN, THE NETHERLANDS – DIAGNOSIS: ASPERGER SYNDROME

"SUPERHEROES, MUM AND DAD, SKYLANDERS AND RED BALL 4. OH, AND LEGO, AND LONDON."

CAMERON, AGE 8, FROM GLASGOW, SCOTLAND

Cameron

Juniper

"DOGS ARE VERY PLAYFUL. THEY LOVE BEING WITH YOU, THEY LOVE SLEEPING WITH YOU, AND THEY'RE GENTLE AND NICE AND I LOVE DOGS! I'M WAITING FOR MY SERVICE DOG. MY FAVOURITE DOGS ARE GERMAN SHEPHERDS AND GOLDEN RETRIEVERS. I HAVE 189 TOY DOGS. I ALSO LOVE TAZOO. HE'S A CAT."

JUNIPER, AGE 7, FROM TORONTO, CANADA – DIAGNOSIS: PREFERS THE TERM "ASPERKID"

"MY DS, WII U TO PLAY POKEMON, SPAGHETTI, AND MY FAMILY."

ESA, AGE 6, FROM LONDON, ENGLAND

Esa

Asher

"ASHER WAS STANDING NEXT TO ME WHEN I
ASKED HIM. HE LOOKED AT ME FOR A MINUTE...
AND THEN I GOT A HEAD HUG.
HE DOESN'T ALWAYS NEED WORDS."

ASHER, AGE 10, FROM COLUMBUS, OHIO, USA
DIAGNOSIS: AUTISM, CHILD APRAXIA OF SPEECH
(ASHER'S MOTHER RUNS THE BLOG AND FACEBOOK PAGE "RUNNING THROUGH WATER".)

"OH, I JUST LOVE
WEARING A PRINCESS DRESS.
IT'S SO BEAUTIFUL!"

LINEA, AGE 3, FROM COPENHAGEN, DENMARK

Linea

Oscar

"I'M DIFFERENT FROM OTHER PEOPLE. I DON'T REALLY KNOW – BEING ABLE TO WIN AWARDS FOR WHAT I'M GOOD AT. BEING GOOD AT VIDEO GAMES, ERM, YEAH."

OSCAR, AGE 12, FROM KENT, ENGLAND – DIAGNOSIS: ASPERGER SYNDROME
(BROTHER OF HENRY ON THE OPPOSITE PAGE)

"IN MATHS, PEOPLE GO FOR THE METHOD
THEY WERE JUST TAUGHT. I CAN SEE
ALL THE DIFFERENT WAYS TO DO IT.
EVERYTHING IS A SHAPE, EVEN NUMBERS."

HENRY, AGE 16, FROM KENT, ENGLAND – DIAGNOSIS: ASPERGER SYNDROME, HIGH SPD
(BROTHER OF OSCAR ON THE OPPOSITE PAGE)

Henry

AJ

"HAVING A FAMILY WHO LOVES ME, READING, AND BEING AUTISTIC — BECAUSE IF I WAS NEUROTYPICAL, I WOULD BE BORING."

AJ, AGE 12, FROM VIRGINIA, USA — DIAGNOSIS: ASD

"PEOPLE WHO MAKE ME HAPPY, LIKE FRIENDS AND FAMILY."

RYAN, AGE 11, FROM RADCLIFFE-ON-TRENT, NOTTINGHAM, ENGLAND

DIAGNOSIS: ASPERGER SYNDROME, ADHD

IN PHOTO: RYAN ACCOMPANIED BY MARK (DAD), RUTH (MUM),
JAMIE (BROTHER) AND EVAN (BEST FRIEND).

Ryan

Josh

"I LIKE MY IPAD, GOOGLE AND MINECRAFT, AND I LOVE YOUTUBE. I ALSO LOVE TV CHANNEL LOGOS. AND FLAGS."

JOSH, AGE 4, FROM CENTRAL COAST, NEW SOUTH WALES, AUSTRALIA

DIAGNOSIS: ASD, EXPRESSIVE LANGUAGE DELAY

"PLAYING OUTSIDE AND WATCHING."
(SHE OFTEN SITS AT THE TOP OF SLIDES,
CLIMBING FRAMES, HILLS, ETC. AND WATCHES
HER SURROUNDINGS. GREAT FOR REDUCING HER
ANXIETY, AND ALLOWS HER TO BECOME
FAMILIAR WITH HER ENVIRONMENT.)

ELIZA, AGE 7, FROM NORTHAMPTONSHIRE, ENGLAND — DIAGNOSIS: ASD
(ELIZA'S MOTHER RUNS A BLOG & FACEBOOK PAGE CALLED "LIVING WITH BLOOMING AUTISM")

Eliza

Riley

"ONE THING THAT GIVES ME GREAT HAPPINESS IS MUSIC."

RILEY, AGE 12, FROM AUSTIN, TEXAS – DIAGNOSIS: ASPERGER SYNDROME

"JOSEPH LOVES MUSIC. ANYTHING IS MUSIC IN JOSEPH'S EARS, AND WHEN HE HEARS A SOUND HE LIKES, HE WILL ASK FOR IT 'AGAIN, AGAIN – MORE, MORE.' HE ONLY HAS TO HEAR SOMETHING ONCE AND HE CAN RECALL EVERY SOUND TO A T. IT'S AMAZING TO WATCH HIM IN ACTION."

JOSEPH, AGE 4, FROM COUNTY DUBLIN, IRELAND – DIAGNOSIS: REGRESSIVE AUTISM

Joseph

Joshua + Bethany

BROTHER & SISTER FROM LINCOLNSHIRE, ENGLAND

"I LOVE TO WATCH AND PLAY FOOTBALL WHEN I'M NOT ON MY COMPUTER."

JOSHUA, AGE 11
DIAGNOSIS: AUTISM, ADHD

"I LOVE ANIMALS AND WANT TO WORK WITH THEM WHEN I'M OLDER. I ALSO LOVE DANCING AND GYMNASTICS."

BETHANY, AGE 8 – DIAGNOSIS: AUTISM

"WATCHING RATED R MOVIES!"

QUINN, AGE 15, FROM GILBERT, ARIZONA, USA — DIAGNOSIS: CLASSIC AUTISM

NOTE: QUINN HAS NEVER ACTUALLY SEEN AN R-RATED MOVIE,
BUT LIKES TO CONSTANTLY MAKE JOKES. HE ESPECIALLY LOVES WORD GAMES
AND BEING SILLY BY SAYING THE OPPOSITE OF WHAT HE IS SUPPOSED TO.
(QUINN IS PICTURED ON WIKIPEDIA'S AUTISM PAGE. HIS MOM DESIGNED THIS BOOK & RUNS MYRIA.COM.)

Quinn

"ICE CREAM!"

RASHEED, AGE 8, FROM ALEXANDRIA, EGYPT — DIAGNOSIS: PDD-NOS

Rasheed

"I LOVE LETTERS THE MOST."

PETER, AGE 4, FROM BREMERTON, WASHINGTON, USA
DIAGNOSIS: AUTISM WITH HYPERLEXIA

Peter

LOVE

Parker

"SOMETIMES YOU FOCUS SO HARD ON HEARING THE WORDS 'I LOVE YOU' THAT YOU OVERLOOK THAT LOVE IS BEING GIVEN. A KISS, A HUG, A SILLY LITTLE GRIN – IT ALL EQUALS LOVE, AND IT IS SUCH A BEAUTIFUL WAY OF EXPRESSING IT! AFTER ALL, LOVE IS A WORD THAT IS MEANT TO BE FELT, NOT HEARD."

PARKER, AGE 4, FROM LONG ISLAND, NEW YORK, USA
DIAGNOSIS: ASD LEVEL 2

"I LOVE TIME THE MOST BECAUSE IT ALLOWS ME TO: SPEND TIME WITH MY DAD, PLAYING COMPUTER GAMES WITH HIM; SPEND TIME PLAYING WITH MY FRIEND, SKIPPING, HULA HOOPING AND SPRINTING; SPEND TIME WITH PONIES LIKE BLUE, PENNY, SWEEP, AND, MOST IMPORTANTLY, ECLIPSE FROM JANET'S YARD; PLAYING YAHTZEE WITH MY MUMMY AND CUDDLING HER. WITHOUT TIME, I WOULD BE A LITTLE ROCK INSTEAD OF A BIG GIANT!"

WILLIAM, AGE 9, FROM WARWICK, ENGLAND – DIAGNOSIS: HFA, PDA

William

"FLOWERS!"

CALVIN, AGE 5, FROM NEW YORK, NEW YORK, USA
DIAGNOSIS: SEVERE AUTISM

Calvin

Daisy

"IF I COULD TALK, I WOULD TELL YOU THAT I LOVE TO LAUGH
AND SMILE. I LOVE BALLS - I LOVE TO THROW THEM AND TO
WATCH THEM DROP DOWN FROM A BUCKET.
I ALSO LOVE BEADS ON A WIRE. I LIKE TO WATCH THEM MOVE
AND LIKE THE SOUND THEY MAKE WHEN THEY CLICK TOGETHER.
I LOVE TO WATCH OCTONAUTS. IT'S THE ONLY PROGRAMME I
WATCH, AND IT MAKES ME LAUGH, ESPECIALLY KWAZII.
I ALSO LOVE MY FAMILY. THEY MAKE ME SMILE AND LAUGH!"

DAISY, AGE 3, FROM MANCHESTER, ENGLAND
DIAGNOSIS: SEVERE AUTISM, DYSPRAXIA AND SPD

43

Ronan

"RONAN LOVES 'HIDE YOUR LOVE AWAY'
(BEATLES VERSION PREFERRED,
BUT PEARL JAM WILL DO IN A PINCH)
AND FINDING THE ORDER IN THE WORLD."

RONAN, AGE 4, FROM WISCONSIN, USA (HIS SISTER EOWYN IS ON THE OPPOSITE PAGE)=

"I LOVE TO PLAY! IT HAS TOYS. LIFE HAS FACES! ALSO EVERYTHING!"

EOWYN, AGE 6, FROM WISCONSIN, USA
(HER BROTHER RONAN IS ON THE OPPOSITE PAGE)

Eowyn

Connor

"LIFE FOR ME IS ENJOYABLE BUT DIFFERENT COMPARED TO OTHER PEOPLE. BEING DIFFERENT IS OK – EVERYONE IS DIFFERENT, BUT NOT EVERYONE IS BRAVE ENOUGH TO ADMIT IT. THE REASONS I LOVE MY LIFE IS BECAUSE I HAVE AN AMAZING FAMILY, GREAT FRIENDS THAT MEAN A LOT TO ME, AND I LOVE VIDEO GAMES AND RESEARCHING DIFFERENT REPTILES, LIKE SNAKES AND LIZARDS. WHEN I'M OLDER, I WANT TO EITHER BE AN ASTROPHYSICIST OR STUDY REPTILES, AND GO 'ROUND THE WORLD AND ENCOUNTER MANY DIFFERENT SPECIES!"

CONNOR, AGE 14, FROM HAMPSHIRE, ENGLAND
DIAGNOSIS: ASPERGER SYNDROME

Milo

Cadence

"I LIKE THAT IT DOESN'T MATTER WHERE ANYONE IS IN THE WORLD, EVERYONE CAN SEE THE SAME MOON. SOMETIMES EVEN AT THE SAME TIME. IT DOESN'T MATTER IF THEY ARE AUTISM OR NOT, OR WHAT COUNTRY THEY ARE FROM OR WHAT COLOUR THEIR SKIN IS, OR IF THEY SPEAK A DIFFERENT LANGUAGE, OR IF THEY DON'T TALK AT ALL. THEY SEE THE SAME MOON AS I SEE. NO ONE HAS TO FEEL LONELY IF THEY CAN SEE THE MOON."

CADENCE, AGE 8, FROM QUEENSLAND, AUSTRALIA – COMMUNICATES NONVERBALLY
CADENCE AND HER FAMILY RUN A WEBSITE AND FACEBOOK PAGE CALLED "I AM CADENCE".

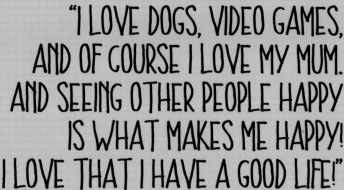

"I LOVE DOGS, VIDEO GAMES, AND OF COURSE I LOVE MY MUM. AND SEEING OTHER PEOPLE HAPPY IS WHAT MAKES ME HAPPY! I LOVE THAT I HAVE A GOOD LIFE!"

Egan

EGAN, AGE 14, FROM OXFORD, ENGLAND
DIAGNOSIS: ASD

Nothing else. This is all Black bush for hair seriously, this is it.

Egan

Random explosion! NEEE EEEEE EEEERD! (kind of)

BECAUSE EGAN'S FACE IS ONLY SEMI-VISIBLE IN THE PHOTO, HERE'S HIS SELF-PORTRAIT TO MAKE UP FOR IT.

49

Ewan

MOM: "WHAT MAKES YOU HAPPY?"
EWAN: "I HAVE NO IDEA."
MOM: "WHAT MAKES YOU SAD?"
EWAN: "PEOPLE SHOUTING AT ME, AND A DEAD PIGEON."
(HE SAW ONE ABOUT TWO YEARS AGO.)
MOM: "WHEN YOU ARE SAD, WHAT MAKES YOU FEEL HAPPY AGAIN?"
EWAN: "FREE ICE CREAM... THE PINK AND WHITE ONE THEY GIVE
ME, AND BWANKIES." (HE OFFERS THEM TO ME TO KEEP ME SAFE OR
FEEL BETTER WHEN I AM ILL.)

EWAN, AGE 8, FROM BOKSBURG, SOUTH AFRICA – DIAGNOSIS: ASPERGER SYNDROME, ADD

"I LIKE OZZY [MY CAT]. I LIKES ROBOTS. RETRO ROBOTS, VINTAGE ROBOTS, ELECTRONIC WALKING ROBOTS, TALKING ROBOTS, ROBOTS FROM EBAY AND AMAZON, EVEN CHEAP ROBOTS. I LIKE MY FAMILY. I LIKE MY FRIENDS. OH. AND ALL KINDS, JUST EVERY KINDS OF ROBOTS."

MADDOX, AGE 10, FROM TEXAS, USA

DIAGNOSIS: ASD, SPD, EPILEPSY, GENERALIZED ANXIETY DISORDER, ADHD

MADDOX'S MOTHER RUNS THE FACEBOOK PAGE "MADDOX'S AUTISM CHRONICLES"

Maddox

"HAVING FRIENDS AND
FAMILY THAT CARE.
FAMILY, INCLUDING PETS.
FOOD WOULD BE MY
SECOND ANSWER."

EVIE, AGE 16
FROM LOUGHBOROUGH,
LEICESTERSHIRE, ENGLAND
DIAGNOSIS: ASD, ANXIETY,
SPD, IRLEN SYNDROME

Evie

"WHEN I ASKED AYDEN 'WHAT DO YOU LOVE?'
HIS RESPONSE WAS 'AYDEN WHAT DO YOU LOVE?'
– SMILING FACE WITH SMILING EYES.
AYDEN LOVES ANYTHING TO DO WITH
ALPHABETS AND NUMBERS. HE LOVES TO READ,
PLAY WITH BUBBLES, DANCE TO BRUNO MARS,
AND VISIT DIFFERENT FARMS."

AYDEN, AGE 3,
FROM QUEENS, NEW YORK, USA
DIAGNOSIS: HF-ASD

Ayden

"I HAVE LOADS OF THINGS I LOVE ABOUT LIFE. ONE IS LIVING. CAN I PUT THAT AND THEN THREE OTHER ANSWERS? HOW MANY ANSWERS ARE YOU ALLOWED? ...NUMBER TWO IS HAVING PEOPLE AROUND ME. HAVING FRIENDS AND FAMILY IS AMAZING. IF YOU DON'T HAVE FRIENDS AND FAMILY THEN TRY AND MAKE SOME. FRIENDS. NOT FAMILY. YOU CAN'T MAKE FAMILY. NUMBER THREE IS DEFINITELY NOT VIDEO GAMES. I LIKE VIDEO GAMES, BUT... NO. I LOVE DAYLIGHT. SPRING IS NICE. NOT JUST THE WORD, THE SEASON AS WELL. I LIKE BOTH. I LIKE USING MY IMAGINATION."

ROBERT, AGE 12, FROM GLASGOW, SCOTLAND
DIAGNOSIS: ASPERGER SYNDROME

Robert

"THE BEST THING ABOUT LIFE IS POLISH SAUSAGE, SWIMMING, HIKING AND DRUMMING! OH, AND DRAWING – I CAN EXPRESS MY FEELINGS WITHOUT WORDS. AND MY FAMILY! THEY ARE EVEN MORE CRAZY THAN I AM."

MICHAEL "JAKE", AGE 9, FROM CYPRUS – DIAGNOSIS: NONVERBAL ASD

MICHAEL'S MOTHER RUNS A BLOG ON ICARE4AUTISM.ORG NAMED "A MOM'S DIARY" AND A FACEBOOK PAGE CALLED "URSA CONSTELLATION OF AUTISM MAMA BEAR"

Michael

Roman

"KNOWING THAT MY MUM AND DAD LOVE ME."

ROMAN, AGE 12, FROM EXETER, DEVON, ENGLAND
ROMAN'S FAMILY RUNS THE FACEBOOK PAGE "CARDS FOR ROMAN"

Clay

"I WAS BORN THIS WAY."

CLAY, AGE 14, FROM BRISBANE, AUSTRALIA
DIAGNOSIS: AUTISM

"WHAT I LOVE IN LIFE IS PLAYING WITH FRIENDS, PLAYING ON PLAYGROUNDS, PLAYDATES WITH COUSINS, WEARING PRETTY CLOTHES, BEING WITH FAMILY, AND HAVING TINY LITTLE PARTIES... HAVING IMAGINARY FRIENDS, PLAYING OUTSIDE PRETENDING MY SWINGSET IS A FAIR, JUMPING ON MY TRAMPOLINE WITH MY SISTER... AND CREATING ART. THAT IS ALL ONE BIG ANSWER."

ALYSSA, AGE 11, FROM WISCONSIN, USA — DIAGNOSIS: AUTISM, SPD

Alyssa

Isaiah

"I LOVE DINOSAURS, W CARS & JAVERT."

ISAIAH, AGE 5, FROM SUSSEX, ENGLAND
(W CARS ARE VWS, AND JAVERT IS A CHARACTER FROM "LES MISERABLES")

Nessa

"READING, WATCHING NETFLIX, READING SOME MORE, GETTING AND GIVING COMPLIMENTS, DOING EVEN MORE READING, PLAYING STRATEGY GAMES WITH MY DAD, LISTENING TO AUDIOBOOKS, AND HANGING FROM MY MOM'S YOGA TRAPEZE. PLUS EVEN MORE READING!"

NESSA, AGE 11, FROM IOWA, USA
DIAGNOSIS: HIGH FUNCTIONING AUTISM

"MY FAMILY. YOUR [MY] MOM, YOUR DAD, YOUR BROTHER, YOUR SISTER. ANNA. AND JAZ. [HIS THERAPISTS] AND DINOSAUR VIDEOS. AND DINOSAURSES. MY FAVOURITE IS THE T-REX AND THE CARNOTAURUS SET. WHAT'S YOUR FAVOURITE? I LIKE THE VIDEOS. AND I'LL GET THE T-REX SKELETON BONES FOR THE NEXT TIME. MAYBE THE ELVES MAKE THAT."

EVAN, AGE 6, FROM NORTHERN VIRGINIA, USA – DIAGNOSIS: ASD, SPD, ANXIETY
EVAN'S MOTHER RUNS A BLOG AND FACEBOOK PAGE CALLED "FROM THE BOWELS OF MOTHERHOOD".

Evan

"JOSEPH IS A VERY HAPPY, AFFECTIONATE AND BOUNCY BOY, WHO LOVES SPINNING, JUMPING, SINGING, OPEN SPACES AND THE COLOUR YELLOW. HE LOVES COOKING BOTH AT HOME AND AT SCHOOL, BECAUSE HE LOVES THE TASTES, TEXTURES, AS WELL AS SEEING HOW THINGS CHANGE WHEN HEATED OR COOLED. HE DOESN'T SAY MANY WORDS, BUT WHEN HE DOES, IT MEANS THE WORLD TO US AND HOLDS GREAT MEANING FOR HIM. HIS FAVOURITE THINGS TO SAY ARE, 'CUDDLE' AND 'BE HAPPY'... WHICH IS A BEAUTIFUL WAY TO EXPRESS JUST WHO OUR JOE IS!"

JOEY, AGE 6, FROM DARLINGTON, ENGLAND — DIAGNOSIS: NONVERBAL ASD

"I THINK WHEN MARLEY GROWS UP, HE WOULD LIKE TO BE THE DICTIONARY. AND A CALCULATOR. AND A TRAIN! WHAT HE LOVES ABOUT LIFE? HE LOVES THE WORLD. AND BEING A BIG BROTHER AND THE JOY OF BEING UTTERLY PRESENT IN THE MOMENT. AND NUMBERS! LOTS OF NUMBERS! ALSO, HE ENJOYS STANDING ON HIS HEAD, THE PERIODIC TABLE, SINGING INDONESIAN SONGS (A RANDOM DISCOVERY!) AND ADORES HIS BABY SISTER GEORGINA. WHEN SHE CRIES, HE WILL COMFORT HER IN ENGLISH, MALAY AND INDONESIAN. IF SHE NEEDS A NAPPY CHANGE, THEN MARLEY IS YOUR MAN."

MARLEY, AGE 6, FROM SINGAPORE — DIAGNOSIS: ASD

Marley

Katherine + Emily + James

SIBLINGS FROM MORAY, SCOTLAND

"MY SHEER ENJOYMENT OF TV SHOWS & VIDEO GAMES."

JAMES, AGE 17

"FOOD – LOTS OF FOOD, AND MY BIRTHDAY, AND CAKE– I LOVE CAKE."

KATHERINE, AGE 13

"I LIKE PLAYING WITH MY TOYS, EATING CHOCOLATE ERMMM,
DRINKING CHOCOLATE MILK, IRN BRU AND COKE, ERRM, I LIKE
BIRTHDAYS ERMM ERMM ERMM, GIGGLING AND BEING A CAT
NAMED MRS NORRIS, AND SITTING IN MY FOUNTAIN AND DIPPING
MARSHMALLOWS IN MY CHOCOLATE FOUNTAIN. I LIKE PARTIES ERMM HUMMMM
AND PLAYING ON MY SCOOTER WHILE BLOWING BUBBLES. THAT IS ALL. THANK YOU."

EMILY, AGE 8

"'I LIKE WATER, PLAY IN THE WATER, SWIMMING. I LIKE CLIMBING."
SINCE BIRTH, EMMETT WAS CAPTIVATED BY NATURE, TREES,
THE OCEAN, AND THE OUTDOORS. THE NATURAL WORLD
SURROUNDING HIM BRINGS SO MUCH JOY INTO HIS LIFE. HE ALSO
LOVES TO SEE AND TO TOUCH ALL TYPES OF ANIMALS.

EMMETT, AGE 6, FROM BOSTON, MASSACHUSETTS, USA
DIAGNOSIS: AUTISM, ADHD, SPD, HAPPINESS
EMMETT'S MOTHER RUNS A FACEBOOK PAGE CALLED "RANTINGS OF AN ADHD MOM"

Freddie

"I KNOW I SHOULD DO THE RIGHT THING AND SAY FAMILY, BUT I WANT TO BE HONEST AND SAY DAYDREAMING! I LOVE DAYDREAMING, AND YOU CAN'T DO THAT IF YOU'RE NOT ALIVE. THE BEST THING ABOUT LIFE IS HOW THERE IS ALWAYS SOMETHING NEW EACH DAY AND YOU CAN'T GET BORED. THERE'S ALWAYS ROOM TO SPREAD YOUR WINGS. NOTHING IS LIMITED WHEN IT COMES TO IMAGINATION. ALL YOU HAVE TO DO IS KNOW YOUR LIMITATIONS AND BREAK THEM!"

FREDDIE, AGE 11, FROM WHITECHAPEL, LONDON, UK – DIAGNOSIS: HF-ASD

"GETTING TO DO FUN STUFF AND BEING WITH MY FAMILY!"

CADE, AGE 9, FROM ALACHUA, FLORIDA, USA
DIAGNOSIS: HFA (HIGH FUNCTIONING AUTISM), ADHD, SPD, ANXIETY,
IDIOPATHIC JUVENILE ARTHRITIS, IMMUNE DEFICIENCY, AND GASTROPARESIS.
NOTHING STOPS THIS SUPER HAPPY KID!

Cade

Harry

"I LOVE HAVING MY PERSONALITY.
ASPERGERS WON'T BREAK ME, IT MAKES ME!"

HARRY, AGE 11, FROM WATERLOOVILLE, PORTSMOUTH, ENGLAND
DIAGNOSIS: ASPERGER SYNDROME, DYSPRAXIA, HYPERMOBILITY

"I ASKED SEBASTIAN WHAT HE LOVED MOST ABOUT LIFE, AND HE LOOKED CONFUSED ABOUT THE QUESTION AND DIDN'T ANSWER ME. SO I WORDED IT DIFFERENTLY BY ASKING HIM WHAT HE LIKED THE MOST OUT OF THREE THINGS HE LOVES: THE ELEVATOR, THE CAR WASH, OR THE METRORAIL. HE SAID, 'METRORAIL. WE GO TO THE METRORAIL NOW.'"

SEBASTIAN, AGE 5, FROM HOUSTON, TEXAS, USA — DIAGNOSIS: AUTISM

Sebastian

Alex

"MY FAVORITE THING IS SCHOOL, BECAUSE I LOVE SCHOOL. DANTA'S (GRANDAD'S) SUNDAY DINNER, SUNDAY SCHOOL, AND PLAYING WITH SAND. CAN I PLAY IN THE SAND NOW?"

ALEX, AGE 7, FROM SOUTH WALES – DIAGNOSIS: AUTISM, GDD
ALEX'S MOTHER RUNS THE FACEBOOK PAGE "WHAT IS 'NORMAL' ANYWAY?"

Mark

Blake

"I LIKE LEGO! I LOVE MY MUM AND DEFINITELY MY BIKE.
I ALSO LOVE MY CATS, MY RABBITS, AND MY CHICKENS.
I LOVE GOING TO OTHER PEOPLES' HOUSES BECAUSE
YOU CAN STROKE OTHER PEOPLES' GUINEA PIGS.
I ENJOY DOING GARDENING. I LOVE PLAYING ON MY
SCOOTER. I LOVE ALL OUR DVDS."

BLAKE, AGE 8, FROM CATTERICK GARRISON, YORKSHIRE, ENGLAND

"MUSIC IS MY BEST FRIEND."

CATARINA, AGE 17, FROM PORTUGAL

Catarina

Aiden

"I LOVE BEING OUTSIDE, PLAYING, AND NEVER COMING INSIDE."

AIDEN, AGE 9, FROM RUGBY, WARWICKSHIRE, ENGLAND
(BROTHER OF HARRISON ON OPPOSITE PAGE)
DIAGNOSIS: ASPERGER SYNDROME, ADHD, GAD
HARRISON AND AIDEN'S FAMILY RUN A FACEBOOK PAGE CALLED "FOGGYSPECTRUM".

"GETTING INTO MY ONESIE
MAKES ME FEEL GOOD."

HARRISON, AGE 11, FROM RUGBY, WARWICKSHIRE, ENGLAND
(BROTHER OF AIDEN ON OPPOSITE PAGE)
DIAGNOSIS: CLASSIC AUTISM, TOURETTES, ADHD

Harrison

Philip

"WHAT I LOVE MOST ABOUT LIFE IS TALKING TO PEOPLE. I TALK ONE LETTER AT A TIME. MY LIFE IS MUCH BETTER NOW THAT I CAN COMMUNICATE THIS WAY. COMMUNICATION MAKES LIFE HAPPY BY CONNECTING PEOPLE AND SHARING OUR THOUGHTS AND FEELINGS."

PHILIP, AGE 13, FROM BUFFALO, NEW YORK, USA
PHILIP PERSONALLY RUNS A BLOG CALLED "FAITH, HOPE, AND LOVE... WITH AUTISM" & ITS FACEBOOK PAGE

"LIGHTNING MCQUEEN, KERR-CHOW! HE'S MY BEST FRIEND."

JOSHUA, AGE 5, FROM WALSALL, WEST MIDLANDS, ENGLAND – DIAGNOSIS: ASD
JOSHUA HAS A LOT OF FRIENDS, BUT LIGHTNING MCQUEEN IS SO SPECIAL TO US ALL.
HE HAS HELPED HIM SO MUCH ON HIS JOURNEY THROUGH LIFE.

Joshua

"THE THING ALEXIA LOVES THE MOST IS HER FAMILY, BUT IF SHE NEEDS TO CHOOSE AN OBJECT, IT'S HER DRAGONS. THIS IS, AND HAS BEEN, HER PASSION SINCE SHE FIRST SAW ONE, AND SHE HAS OVER A HUNDRED NOW, IN PLUSH OR PLASTIC."

ALEXIA, AGE 9, FROM AARHUS, DENMARK
DIAGNOSIS: ASPERGER SYNDROME

"SNUGGLING WITH MY BLANKIE AND YOU, MOMMY. AND I LIKE MINECRAFT BECAUSE IT'S MADE OUT OF BLOCKS. AND I LIKE MY DOG BECAUSE SHE STEALS MY BLANKIE."

BRYCE, AGE 9, FROM CHARLOTTE, NORTH CAROLINA, USA

Bryce

Brandon

BRANDON: "I LIKE COMPUTERS THE MOST ABOUT LIFE."
ME: "ANYTHING ELSE?"
BRANDON: "NO."

BRANDON, AGE 8, FROM CHESTERFIELD, ENGLAND – DIAGNOSIS: ASD

"WHAT I LOVE MOST ABOUT LIFE IS HAVING MY FAMILY TO LOOK OUT FOR ME, MINECRAFT, LEGO, AND MINECRAFT LEGO!"

JAKE, AGE 12, FROM REDCAR, TEESSIDE, ENGLAND

Jake

Jadyn + Isabel + Kyle

SIBLINGS FROM SINGAPORE

"MY FAMILY!"

JADYN, AGE 12 – DIAGNOSIS: ASPERGER SYNDROME

"DANCE, BECAUSE I CAN EXPRESS MYSELF
IN ANOTHER WAY OTHER THAN WORDS."

ISABEL, AGE 15 – DIAGNOSIS: ASPERGER SYNDROME

"BEING ABLE TO HELP OTHERS AND TOUCH LIVES.

(HE WANTS TO BE A PSYCHOLOGIST/EVANGELIST/PASTOR WHEN HE GROWS UP.)

KYLE, AGE 16 – DIAGNOSIS: ASPERGER SYNDROME

"WHAT I LOVE MOST ABOUT LIFE IS WAKING UP FROM A DREAM – BUT YOU KNOW I NEVER SLEEP, BUT YEAH, YOU KNOW WHAT I MEAN? ANYWAY, WAKING UP FROM A DREAM AND WRITING AND DRAWING MY OWN MINECRAFT SECRETS BOOKS AND STUFF. IT'S MY FAVOURITE THING BECAUSE I CAN THINK UP THINGS IN MY HEAD AND DRAW THEM, AND WRITE THEM DOWN... I HAVE SO MANY GREAT IDEAS IN MY BRAIN. OH, AND PLAYING GAMES OF COURSE!"

JUDE, AGE 8, FROM BIGGAR, SCOTLAND – DIAGNOSIS: ASD

"MY PHONE. ALSO VIDEO GAMES. ALSO LEGO. ALSO TV. ALSO COMPUTERS. ALSO PLAYING MINECRAFT ON MY PHONE. ALSO LEATHER AND SOFTNESS. AND THE NATIONAL SPACE CENTRE, BECAUSE I GET TO FIDDLE WITH EVERYTHING AND PUSH ALL THE BUTTONS, AND I CAN'T DO THAT NORMALLY!"

DANIEL, AGE 8, FROM RADCLIFFE-ON-TRENT, NOTTINGHAM, ENGLAND – DIAGNOSIS: ASD, ADHD

Daniel

PHOTO: SARAH WILKES PHOTOGRAPHY

84

Alex

"I LOVE TO SPEND TIME WITH MY FAMILY,
PLAY VIDEO GAMES, PLAY WITH MY SISTER,
AND PLAY WITH MY BIONICLES. I LIKE TO PLAY
IN MY MIND WORLD – WHERE MY BIONICLES
AND CHARACTERS I CREATE CAN DO BATTLE."

ALEX, AGE 15, FROM NORTHERN NEW JERSEY, USA
DIAGNOSIS: AUTISM, PERVASIVE DEVELOPMENTAL DELAY

Rowan

"I ASKED MY LITTLE BOY WHAT HIS FAVOURITE THIN
[LI]FE WAS. HE IS A TOTAL STAR WARS FANATIC, SO I
[EX]PECTED THE ANSWER TO MATCH THAT. HE ANSWER[ED]
[WI]TH TWO WORDS. HE SAID 'YOU' AND THEN 'FAMILY,'
[AND] THEN, 'DO YOU ASK THAT QUESTION TO ALL YOUR
[KID]S?' WHEN I TOLD HIM ABOUT THE BOOK, HE SAID, 'OH
[I C]OULD HAVE SAID FOOTBALL!'"

[ROW]AN, AGE 9 FROM WESTERN AUSTRALIA – DIAGNOSIS: ASD

"THE THING I LOVE THE MOST ABOUT LIFE IS SKATEBOARDING!"

TYE, AGE 12, FROM SOUTH FLORIDA, USA
DIAGNOSIS: ASPERGER SYNDROME

Tye

"I LUB IT, DE IPAD."

LUCKY, AGE 5, FROM HAMPSHIRE, ENGLAND (BROTHER OF BEAR ON OPPOSITE PAGE)
DIAGNOSIS: PDA, LANGUAGE DISORDER
LUCKY AND BEAR'S MOTHER RUNS A FACEBOOK PAGE NAMED "WE CALLED HIM LUCKY"

Lucky

Bear

"I LIKE BEING WITH MUMMY, AND I LIKE PLAYING CHESS!"

BEAR, AGE 7, FROM HAMPSHIRE, ENGLAND (BROTHER OF LUCKY ON OPPOSITE PAGE)

DIAGNOSIS: ASD, ADHD

Sherin

"MY MYSTERIOUS JOURNEY WITH MY AUTISM IS WHAT I LOVE MOST ABOUT MY LIFE. IT MAKES ME LOOK LIKE A SUPERHERO AND A STUPID AT THE SAME TIME. MOST PEOPLE THINK I REALLY DO NOT HAVE ANY GOALS IN MY LIFE BUT SURE I DO HAVE A WISH. WRITING GIVES WINGS TO MY THOUGHTS. MY AUTISM GIVES MY PEN THE POWER TO USE MY SO-CALLED DISABILITY TO ENABLE MY FELLOW BEINGS TO LIVE A MEANINGFUL LIFE. OUR WORLD BECOMES ONLY RICHER BY THE THOUGHTS OF AUTISTIC PEOPLE."

SHERIN, AGE 14, FROM KERALA, INDIA – DIAGNOSIS: ASD
SHERIN RUNS A WEBSITE CALLED "MUSINGS OF SHERIN" (MUSINGSOFSHER.IN)

"I LIKE ART, I LIKE BASKETBALL, BENCHBALL AND BADMINTON. I LIKE THAT I'M DIFFERENT, I'M NOT BORING. I AM A GOOD FRIEND, I'M GOOD AT UNDERSTANDING AND I HAVE A GREAT SENSE OF SMELL."

PIPPA, AGE 10, FROM RADCLIFFE-ON-TRENT, ENGLAND

DIAGNOSIS: AUTISM, ADHD, DCD, SPD

Pippa

"TWO THINGS THAT ARE IMPORTANT TO ME IN MY LIFE ARE HOCKEY AND MY FARM. HOCKEY IS NOT JUST ABOUT SCORING GOALS. IT'S ABOUT TEAMWORK, AND HAVING FUN, AND NOT JUST SAYING 'WE WON, WE WON AND YOU GUYS LOST'. ALWAYS AT THE END OF THE GAME YOU ALWAYS HAVE TO GO AND SHAKE HANDS, AND THAT'S ALWAYS GOOD. AND ALSO, FARMING IS ABOUT TAKING CARE OF YOUR ANIMALS, AND KEEPING A GOOD FARM AND MAKING SURE NOTHING EVER DIES, LIKE TREES OR GOOD FIELDS. IN THE SPRINGTIME WHEN MY PAPA GOES TO MAKE HAY BALES, I USUALLY GO WITH HIM 'COS IT'S REALLY FUN. SO THOSE ARE THE THINGS THAT ARE IMPORTANT TO ME IN MY LIFE."

JAXON, AGE 10, FROM ALBERTA, CANADA – DIAGNOSIS: PDD-NOS & COMBINED TYPE ADHD

Jaxon

"SOLVING THE IMPOSSIBLE
MYSTERY THAT GIVES
OUR LIVES MEANING."
(FIN ALSO LIKES JUMPING
AROUND IN HIS UNDERWEAR.)

Fin

FIN, AGE 11, FROM CARDIFF, WALES
DIAGNOSIS: ASPERGER SYNDROME

Elijah

"I LOVE ALL ANIMALS!"

ELIJAH, AGE 9, FROM FLORIDA, USA

"I LOVE SWIMMING DOWN THE RAPIDS! AND DIGGING IN THE SAND!"

SASHA, AGE 9, FROM LONDON, ENGLAND – DIAGNOSIS: ASD, PDA

SASHA'S MOTHER RUNS A WEBSITE CALLED "STEPH'S TWO GIRLS", AND A FACEBOOK PAGE OF THE SAME NAME

Sasha

Aidan

"IT'S A HARD ONE TO ANSWER AS HIS SPEECH ISN'T SO ADVANCED TO ANSWER IT, BUT IN LIFE, HE SEEMS TO LOVE CUDDLES, NUMBERS, RAA RAA THE NOISY LION AND TASTY CHICKEN NUGGETS MORE THAN ANYTHING!"

AIDAN, AGE 4, FROM CHESHIRE, ENGLAND – DIAGNOSIS: ASD

"WHAT I LOVE MOST ABOUT LIFE IS PLAYING WITH MY THOMAS AND FRIENDS TOYS."

JUAN MANUEL, AGE 9, FROM BERAZATEGUI, BUENOS AIRES, ARGENTINA
DIAGNOSIS: ASD, WITH SOME SENSORY PROCESSING ISSUES

Juan Manuel

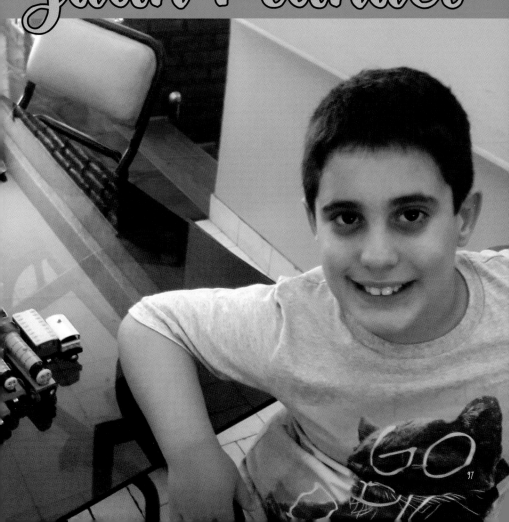

Amanda

"YOU SHOULD APPRECIATE
THE PEOPLE WHO SUPPORT YOU.
THEY ARE THE BEST THINGS IN LIFE."

AMANDA, AGE 16, FROM SIERRA VISTA, ARIZONA, USA
DIAGNOSIS: ASPERGER SYNDROME, ADHD, OCD

"ADAM, ARE YOU HAPPY WITH YOUR LIFE?"
"YES."
"WHAT WOULD YOU CHANGE TO MAKE YOU HAPPIER?"
"LESS PEAS, MORE ROLLERCOASTERS."

ADAM, AGE 10, FROM DEWSBURY, WEST YORKSHIRE, ENGLAND

Adam

Dryden + Cooper

BROTHERS FROM WINDSOR, ONTARIO, CANADA

"WHEN I ASKED HIM 'WHAT DO YOU LIKE MOST ABOUT LIFE?' HE JUST TOUCHED MY FACE AND SMILED. HE DOESN'T OFTEN SAY MUCH, BUT NO WORDS ARE NEEDED TO CONVEY THE BOND BETWEEN US."

DRYDEN, AGE 5 – DIAGNOSIS: MODERATE-TO-SEVERE AUTISM, GDD

"WHEN ASKED 'WHAT DO YOU LIKE MOST ABOUT LIFE,' HE RESPONDED, 'IT'S TIME FOR BIRTHDAY CAKE!'"

COOPER, AGE 4 – DIAGNOSIS: MODERATE-TO-SEVERE AUTISM, GDD

ALSO IN PHOTO: LITTLE BROTHER LENNON, AGE 2
DIAGNOSIS: MILD TO MODERATE ASD

"HASSAAN LOVES CELEBRATIONS. EVERY DAY HE ASKS ME TO GO TO A PARTY. HE LOVES TO SMILE, TO STAY HAPPY AND TO HAVE FUN. NO MATTER WHAT CHALLENGES LIFE HAS THROWN IN THE WAY OF THIS LITTLE BOY, HE KNOW HE CAN WIN EVERYTHING JUST WITH A SMILE. HE TAUGHT ME THAT LIFE IS VERY SHORT AND VERY UNPREDICTABLE SO JUST LIVE, LOVE AND LAUGH."

HASSAAN, AGE 4, FROM LAHORE, PAKISTAN – DIAGNOSIS: REGRESSIVE AUTISM

Hassaan

Oliver

"MUMMY AND DADDY AND CHOCOLATE AND MATHS AND THE SOFA AND ELECTRONICS AND THE BEANO AND BASICALLY EVERYTHING ABOUT MY BEDROOM EXCEPT ZOE'S THINGS!"

OLIVER, AGE 8, FROM BUCKINGHAMSHIRE, ENGLAND
DIAGNOSIS: ASPERGER SYNDROME

"MY FAVOURITE THING IN LIFE IS THE CHILDREN'S MUSEUM BECAUSE IT'S AWESOME. CAN I GO NOW?"

KYLIE, AGE 8, FROM CHICAGO, ILLINOIS, USA

Kylie

Beth

"AS AN AUTISTIC AND A MASSIVE WALLFLOWER, YOU OFTEN NOTICE WHAT NO ONE ELSE NOTICES. AND THOSE SMALL DETAILS ARE OFTEN THE DIFFERENCE BETWEEN SHRUGGING MOST THINGS OFF AND TRULY APPRECIATING EVERYTHING AROUND YOU. SO I POSE ANOTHER QUESTION: WHAT'S NOT TO LOVE? OTHER THAN THE FACT THAT FREDDOS NOW COST 20P."

BETH, AGE 13, FROM CORNWALL, ENGLAND – DIAGNOSIS: ASD
(FREDDOS ARE FROG-SHAPED CHOCOLATE BARS)

"I LOVE MY FAMILY AND FRIENDS AND FOOD. AND SOON I WILL INVENT THINGS WHICH I WILL REALLY LOVE. THE FINAL THINGS THAT I LOVE ARE DOGS."

BRENNAN, AGE 10, FROM SHREWSBURY, MASSACHUSETTS, USA — DIAGNOSIS: AUTISM

Brennan

105

Hayden

"1. GETTING TO HAVE NICE FRIENDS WHO HELP ME WHEN I'M HURT AND THINK OF GOOD GAMES; 2. GETTING TO PLAY COOL SPORT; 3. HAVING A BEAUTIFUL FAMILY; 4. HAVING A LOVELY DAD AND MUM 3 MY SISTERS."

HAYDEN, AGE 10
FROM VICTORIA, AUSTRALIA
DIAGNOSIS: HFA

HAYDEN HAS BEEN PLAYING AUSTRALIAN RULES FOOTBALL IN THE UNDER 10'S FOR THE FIRST TIME THIS YEAR. THIS PHOTO IS FROM THE WEEK HE WAS CHOSEN TO BE CAPTAIN. THEY ALSO WON.

"WHEN I TOLD HIM ABOUT THIS BOOK, HE INSISTED HE WEAR HIS LEGO MOVIE 'AWESOME' T-SHIRT. WHEN I ASKED IF HE'D LIKE TO SAY ANYTHING, HE SAID, 'AUTISM MAKES ME GOOD AT COMPUTER GAMES, BUT NOT SO GOOD AT MATH. IT MAKES ME NOT LIKE LOTS OF PEOPLE, BUT I LOVE PUPPIES.'"

Aaron

AARON, AGE 9, FROM TEXAS, USA
DIAGNOSIS: AUTISM, SPD, ANXIETY

Zack

"I LOVE MY FAMILY AND FRIENDS, AND IN MY SPARE TIME, MORE THAN ANYTHING I LIKE WATCHING YOUTUBE GAMING VIDEOS OR DRAWING. I'M PROUD OF BEING AUTISTIC BECAUSE ONE OF MY HEROES, SATOSHI TAJIRI, WHO CREATED POKÉMON, IS AUTISTIC AS WELL. I ALSO LOVE GOING TO LONDON."

ZACK, AGE 12, FROM ÖREBRO, SWEDEN
DIAGNOSIS: AUTISM

"MY FRIENDS AND FAMILY MAKE ME HAPPY."

MELON, AGE 7, FROM BIRMINGHAM, ENGLAND
DIAGNOSIS: AUTISM
(MELON'S MOTHER RUNS A BLOG CALLED "CAT ON A TRAMPOLINE" AND ITS FACEBOOK PAGE)

Melon

Joshua

"I LOVE LIFE IT'S A TREAT
I LOVE LIFE NEW PEOPLE YOU MEET
I LOVE LIFE YOU GET TO PLAY
I LOVE LIFE HIP HIP HOORAY.
BUT WHAT MAKES THAT HAPPEN...
MY FAMILY, PS3 AND ME."

JOSHUA CHOOSES TO WRITE MOST OF HIS THINGS AS POETRY,
AND USES THIS STYLE OF WRITING TO RELEASE HIS EMOTIONS.

JOSHUA, AGE 9, FROM BEECHDALE, NOTTINGHAM, ENGLAND – DIAGNOSIS: HF-ASD

"BLANKETS, BECAUSE YOU CAN SNUGGLE UP IN THEM, YOU (MOMMY), HUGS, DINOSAURS!, AND FLYING REPTILES LIKE THE DRACO LIZARD. THAT'S IT, MOM. JUST PUT A PERIOD AND POST IT!" (HE WANTED TO GET BACK TO WATCHING HIS FAVOURITE SHOW.)

KANAAN, AGE 7, FROM PHOENIX, ARIZONA, USA – DIAGNOSIS: ASPERGER SYNDROME, ADHD

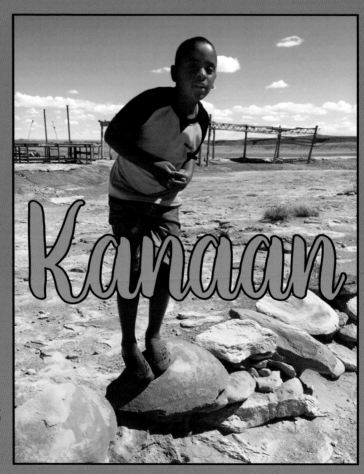

KANAAN WANTED THIS TO BE HIS PHOTO FOR THE BOOK. HE IS STANDING ON FOSSILISED DINOSAUR POO.

Darcey

"I LOVE JUMPING IN MUDDY PUDDLES,
BECAUSE I AM LIKE PEPPA PIG."

DARCEY, AGE 4, FROM EAST SUSSEX, ENGLAND

"IT'S CONFUSING TO TALK ABOUT BECAUSE YOU HAVE FAMILY, POSSESSIONS, FRIENDS... AND THEY CAN ALL BE YOUR FAVOURITE THINGS AT DIFFERENT TIMES."

TULLY, AGE 11, FROM SUNSHINE COAST, QUEENSLAND, AUSTRALIA
DIAGNOSIS: ASPERGER SYNDROME

Tully

FROM MUM:
YOU MAY NOTICE HIS HAIR IN HIS PHOTOS, WE CALL IT 'BARRY'. ONE DAY WHEN HE WAS 7 AND I WAS TRYING TO BRUSH HIS HAIR, I COMMENTED THAT IT HAD A MIND ALL OF ITS OWN. WITHOUT MISSING A BEAT, HE REPLIED, "YEP, ITS NAME IS BARRY, AND HE KNOWS KARATE!"

Bryce

"VIDEO GAMES. THEY'RE FUN! BEING IN PLAYS.
IT'S FUN! AND BECAUSE YOU GET TO ACT OUT
THE MOVIE AND BE A PERSON FROM IT."

BRYCE, AGE 7, FROM CHICO, CALIFORNIA – DIAGNOSIS: PDD-NOS

"THE THINGS I LOVE MOST ABOUT LIFE ARE TAKING TRIPS TO FLORIDA OR TO SOMEWHERE ELSE, RUNNING FAST AND DOING RACES, SWIMMING IN MY POOL, READING BOOKS, OR READING MY IPAD, PLAYING XBOX GAMES, CARS... CARS ARE MY FAVOURITE THING, MY MOMMY AND DADDY, AND REEF [LITTLE BROTHER]. I LOVE JETT [THE DOG], BUT I DO NOT LOVE GAGA [THE CAT]. GAGA IS STUPID."

TOWNES, AGE 7, FROM ARKANSAS, USA

Townes

Kayla

"BEING AT HOME WITH MY FAMILY, WHERE I FEEL SAFE. OH, AND HORSES! BEING WITH HORSES MAKES ME HAPPY!"

KAYLA, AGE 6, FROM ISLE OF MAN – DIAGNOSIS: AUTISM, PDA

KAYLA'S MOTHER RUNS A FACEBOOK PAGE CALLED "PDA HEARTS AND STARS"

"I LOVE AMMI [MOTHER]."
"OTHER THAN AMMI, WHAT DO YOU LOVE?"
"I LOVE CRICKET."

MOHAMMED FUZAIL, AGE 9, FROM MUSCAT, OMAN
DIAGNOSIS: AUTISM

Mohammed Fuzail

117

BROTHERS FROM
OKLAHOMA, USA

Orion + Sam

"THE THING I LOVE MOST ABOUT LIFE IS WHEN YOU DISCOVER SOMETHING AND IT BLOWS YOUR MIND. LIKE FINDING OUT HOW RAINBOWS ARE MADE. AND MAKING A BATTERY OUT OF POTATOES. STUFF LIKE THAT. AND MY FAVOURITE GAME IS LEGENDS OF ZELDA AND MY LEAST FAVOURITE IS FIVE NIGHTS AT FREDDY'S. AND I HAVE CHICKENS. MY FAVOURITE COLOUR IS BLUE AND MY FAVOURITE CHICKEN IS RUSTY [PICTURED]."

ORION, AGE 9
DIAGNOSIS: ASPERGER SYNDROME

"I LOVE WRITING. IN THE PAST SEVEN YEARS, I HAVE DRAWN AND DEVELOPED MANY CHARACTERS: MONSTERS, SUPERHEROES, VILLAINS, PROTAGONISTS, NARRATORS, MUTANTS, AND ALIENS. I HAVE WRITTEN MANY SHORT STORIES INVOLVING THEM. PRESENTLY I AM WRITING MY FIRST NOVEL, WHICH CONNECTS A COUPLE OF MY STORIES AND WILL HAVE SPIN-OFFS. I'M ALSO EAGERLY IMPATIENTLY AWAITING THE FOURTH SEASON OF ROOSTER TEETH'S HIT INTERNET ANIME SERIES RWBY."

SAM, AGE 17
DIAGNOSIS: ASPERGER SYNDROME

"IF SHE'S OUTSIDE, SHE'S HAPPY. IF THERE'S WATER, MUD AND JUMPING, EVEN BETTER!"

FREYA, AGE 4, FROM BIRMINGHAM, ENGLAND – DIAGNOSIS: ASD
FREYA'S FAMILY RUNS A BLOG AND FACEBOOK PAGE CALLED "IT'S A TINK THING".

Freya

Luke

"I LIKE THE SCIENCE MUSEUM.
I WANT SADIE TO GO TO THE SCIENCE MUSEUM."
(SADIE IS A GIRL IN HIS CLASS)

LUKE, AGE 4, FROM FLORIDA, USA
THIS PHOTO IS SPECIAL BECAUSE IT IS ONLY RECENTLY THAT LUKE HAS BEEN ABLE TO ENJOY
PARACHUTE PLAY. SINCE HE WAS AN INFANT, HE WAS ALWAYS BEEN SCARED OF THE PARACHUTE.
THROUGH THE DEDICATED, KIND AND UNDERSTANDING TEACHERS AT HIS SCHOOL, HE HAS THRIVED
AND IS ABLE TO ENJOY MANY THINGS HE ONCE FOUND SCARY.

"I LIKE THE ADVENTURES YOU GET TO HAVE AND THE CHOICES YOU GET TO MAKE. YOU CAN CHOOSE WHO YOU WANT TO BE— IT'S LIKE READING AN ADVENTURE BOOK OR CREATING YOUR OWN GAME. THE BEST THING IS YOU CAN GET INSPIRED BY STUFF... LIKE YOU CAN WATCH SONIC AND THINK 'I WANT TO BE FAST LIKE HIM', OR WWE AND THINK 'I WANT TO ACT AS WELL AS THEY CAN'."

MORGAN, AGE 12, FROM SUDBURY, SUFFOLK, ENGLAND
DIAGNOSIS: ASPERGER SYNDROME, ANXIETY
MORGAN'S MOTHER RUNS A FACEBOOK PAGE CALLED "PLANET MORGAN ASPIE SUPERHERO"

Morgan

FROM CHRIS:
THIS PICTURE WAS TAKEN THE DAY I TOOK HIM TO LONDON. HAVING KNOWN HIM SINCE HE WAS ALMOST TOO ANXIOUS TO LEAVE THE HOUSE, WATCHING HIM HANDLE THE LONDON UNDERGROUND WITH THIS SMILE WAS ONE OF MY FAVOURITE MOMENTS WITH HIM.

Annalise

"MY SPECIAL INTEREST IS DISNEY
AT THE MOMENT, AND I ALSO ENJOY
PHOTOGRAPHY IN MY SPARE TIME."

ANNALISE, AGE 16, FROM HAMPSHIRE, ENGLAND
DIAGNOSIS: HF-ASD

"I LOVE YOU, MAMA, AND EVERYONE. I'M FASCINATED WITH EVERYTHING, LIKE THE PERIODIC TABLE OF THE ELEMENTS. I'M GOING TO BE AN ASTRONAUT. HAVE YOU HEARD OF ELECTRONS? THEY ARE NEGATIVELY CHARGED."

ZEKE (OTHERWISE KNOWN AS TATER), AGE 6, FROM INDIANA, USA – DIAGNOSIS: ASD

Zeke

"BANANAS.
I LIKE BANANAS...
AND HUGS MAKE
ME HAPPY."

JAZPER, AGE 5
DIAGNOSIS: ASD

"WHAT I LOVE
MOST ABOUT LIFE
IS HOW COLOURFUL
IT CAN BE."

DEXTER, AGE 12
DIAGNOSIS: ASPERGER SYNDROME

Dexter
+
Jazper

BROTHERS FROM NEW BRUNSWICK, CANADA
DEXTER AND JAZPER'S PARENTS RUN THE FACEBOOK PAGE "AUSOME SHARPE"

Jack

"I LOVE MY FAMILY AND THE OCEAN. THE SMELL OF THE SEA AND BEING IN THE WATER MAKES ME HAPPY."

JACK, AGE 10, FROM BRISBANE, AUSTRALIA – DIAGNOSIS: AUTISM

125

Harrison + Oscar-Bentley

BROTHERS FROM GLASGOW, SCOTLAND

"FAMILY, VIDEO GAMES, FRIENDS AND THE WORLD – THE WORLD IS DESTINED TO ME!"
– HARRISON, AGE 7

"LEGO, DUPLO, FIRE ENGINES & TOY STORY."
– OSCAR-BENTLEY, AGE 3

"SPLASHING IN THE BLUE SEA!"

EDWARD, AGE 8, FROM BEDFORDSHIRE, ENGLAND

Edward

Leilani

"WHAT LEILANI LOVES THE MOST ABOUT LIFE IS ENJOYING NEW EXPERIENCES WHILE SPREADING AUTISM ACCEPTANCE. IT'S ALWAYS BEEN IMPORTANT FOR US TO HAVE LEILANI EXPERIENCE LIFE TO THE FULLEST, DESPITE HER DIFFERENT ABILITIES. WE ARE NOT ASHAMED OF HER AUTISM, AND WE SPREAD ACCEPTANCE WHEREVER WE GO."

LEILANI, AGE 11, FROM MARYLAND, USA – DIAGNOSIS: AUTISM (NONVERBAL), SPD
LEILANI'S MOTHER RUNS THE WEBSITE AND FACEBOOK PAGE "WALK ONE DAY IN OUR SHOES".

"IF OUR SON WAS ABLE TO VERBALLY EXPRESS HIS FEELINGS, THIS IS WHAT HE MOST PROBABLY WOULD SAY: 'I LOVE MUSIC AND SOMETIMES WISH I COULD ACTUALLY LIVE IN A SONG. BUT NOT ALL SONGS, BECAUSE SOME MUSIC DRIVES ME CRAZY, AND I WOULD FEEL IMPRISONED IF I LIVED IN THESE. I CAN'T EXPLAIN WHICH SONGS I LOVE AND WHICH ONES I HATE.'"

Raúl

RAUL, AGE 4,
FROM AMSTERDAM, THE NETHERLANDS
DIAGNOSIS: ASD

Tyler

"EVERYTHING FUN! BUT NOT SCHOOL, BECAUSE THAT'S NOT FUN."

TYLER, AGE 7, FROM NEW YORK, USA – DIAGNOSIS: ASD

"I LOVE MY FRIENDS AND FAMILY. I AM NOT POPULAR, BUT I HAVE SIX FRIENDS, SO I CAN'T COMPLAIN. I LOVE MY FAMILY. I HAVE ONE MOTHER, ONE FATHER, THREE BROTHERS, ONE NEPHEW AND THREE COUSINS. I AM GREAT WITH BABIES AND CHILDREN. I WILL BE STUDYING CHILD DEVELOPMENT AT COLLEGE. I HOPE TO MOVE TO SWEDEN WHEN I AM OLDER AND START A FAMILY. MY FAVOURITE THINGS ARE SWEDISH, BECAUSE MOST OF THE THINGS I LOVE COME FROM SWEDEN. THESE INCLUDE IKEA, ABBA, AND YOUTUBE VLOGGER PEWDIEPIE. I ALSO LOVE SIMS AND POKÉMON, BUT THESE ARE NOT SWEDISH!"

KERENZA, AGE 16
FROM TAUNTON, ENGLAND
DIAGNOSIS: ASPERGER SYNDROME

Kerenza

Zachary

"THE THING THAT I LOVE MOST ABOUT MY LIFE IS DOING MAGIC. WHAT MADE ME GET INVOLVED WAS A BIRTHDAY PARTY WITH A MAGICIAN. I ALSO LIKE MARTIAL ARTS BECAUSE I LIKE LEARNING COOL MOVES, AND I USE WEAPONS LIKE THE BO STAFF. THOSE ARE THE THINGS I LIKE MOST ABOUT MY LIFE."

ZACHARY, AGE 13, FROM VANCOUVER, WASHINGTON, USA
DIAGNOSIS: AUTISM

"CANDY, TOYS, HALLOWEEN OUTFITS AND HALLOWEEN SURPRISES."
(THIS QUOTE WAS GIVEN IN MARCH.)

TALIA, AGE 6, FROM MANCHESTER, ENGLAND
DIAGNOSIS: AUTISM, SPD

Shemi

"YOU [MOM], FAMILY, MILITARY MILITARY MILITARY AND SPAGHETTI!"

SHEMI, AGE 11, FROM SANTA CRUZ, ARUBA

DIAGNOSIS: ASD WITH MGDD LEVEL 1

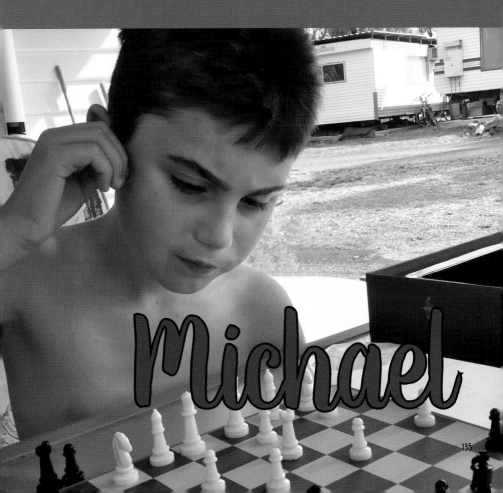

"WHITEBOARDS!"
"WHY DO YOU LIKE THEM?"
"I DON'T LIKE THEM, I LOVE THEM!"

MICHAEL, AGE 8, FROM MELBOURNE, AUSTRALIA
DIAGNOSIS: AUTISM, MILD INTELLECTUAL DISABILITY

HE IS ALWAYS DOING SOMETHING ON HIS WHITEBOARDS LIKE HIS DAILY WRITING OF THE DAY, MONTH, YEAR, TIME AND
WEATHER! THEN HE GOES ON TO WRITE A TIMETABLE FOR HIS DAY. HIS MUM WISHES SHE WERE THAT ORGANISED.

Michael

Scott

"LIFE. I MAY AS WELL ENJOY IT WHILE I'M HERE. IF I WASN'T ALIVE, I'D BE DEAD!"

LOOKING FOR MORE CLARIFICATION, I THEN ASKED HIM WHAT HE COULDN'T LIVE WITHOUT. "INTERNET," WAS HIS ONLY REPLY. GUESS HE'S EASILY PLEASED. THE MOST IMPORTANT THINGS TO HIM ARE FAMILY AND BEING HAPPY. HE IS GENERALLY HAPPY AND CAREFREE. HE DOESN'T UNDERSTAND DISHONESTY OR VIOLENCE BECAUSE HE SAYS THEY SERVE NO PURPOSE AND DON'T SOLVE ANYONE'S PROBLEMS. THE PERSON HE MOST ADMIRES IN THE WORLD IS HIS BIG BROTHER RYAN.

SCOTT, AGE 14, FROM GLASGOW, SCOTLAND – DIAGNOSIS: ASPERGER SYNDROME

"I LOVE BEING ME AND I LIKE DOING THINGS AND LOVE PLAYING WITH FRIENDS AND MAKING FRIENDS, BUT MOST OF ALL I LIKE TO BE WITH MY FAMILY."

PHOEBE, AGE 9, FROM DERBYSHIRE, ENGLAND

DIAGNOSIS: ASD

Phoebe

"WHAT LILY LOVES ABOUT LIFE IS
BEING ACCEPTED AS SHE IS."

LILY, AGE 4, FROM LAKE ARROWHEAD, MAINE, USA
DIAGNOSIS: ASD, SEVERE SPEECH DISORDER

Lily

138

Athen

"ATHEN LOVES EVERYTHING TRAINS!
HE ALSO LOVES COOKING."

ATHEN, AGE 6, FROM COLUMBUS, OHIO, USA
DIAGNOSIS: ASD (LIMITED VERBAL)

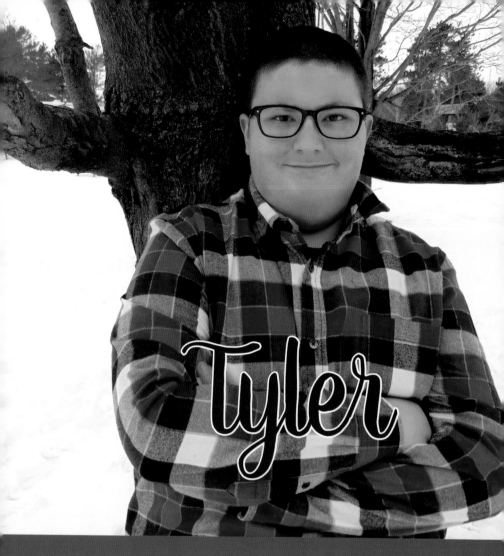

Tyler

"THE FACT THAT THINGS WILL ALWAYS GET BETTER."

TYLER, AGE 14, FROM ONTARIO, CANADA

TYLER'S MOTHER RUNS A FACEBOOK PAGE CALLED "ASPIEMOM: ADVENTURES IN AUTISMLAND"

"STORMTROOPERS!"

SAMUEL, AGE 7, FROM SHEFFIELD, SOUTH YORKSHIRE, ENGLAND — DIAGNOSIS: ASD
HE MET THE STORMTROOPERS AT COMICCON NOT LONG AGO.
IT WAS THE HAPPIEST DAY OF HIS LIFE!

Samuel

"LOADS.
EATING KINDER EGGS.
FLOWERS!
ARROWS. BECAUSE
CARS FOLLOW THEM.
PEACOCKS!
I LOVE PEACOCKS.
I LOVE PEACOCKS.
I LOVE PEACOCKS.
THEY MAKE THE
'ARK' NOISES.
I LOVE FLOWERS.
AND PAVEMENT.
I LOVE BUMPY
PAVEMENTS.
I SPIN ON THEM."

ELIJAH, AGE 9
FROM COVENTRY, ENGLAND
DIAGNOSIS: AUTISM

Elijah

"WHAT I LOVE THE MOST ABOUT LIFE IS HOW EVERYTHING MAKES PERFECT SENSE ONCE YOU STUDY IT AND UNDERSTAND IT. EVERYTHING CAN BE RATIONALLY EXPLAINED BY SCIENCE. I LOVE HOW MIND-BLOWING SCIENCE IS, AND HOW AMAZING THE UNIVERSE AND EVERYTHING IN IT IS. THE WAY OUR CELLS FORM TISSUE, HOW OUR BRAINS PROCESS INFORMATION, HOW COMPLEX THE HUMAN BODY IS. I LOVE LOGIC. I WANT THINGS TO MAKE SENSE I WANT TO UNDERSTAND IT ALL."

Marco

MARCO, AGE 13
FROM NORTHEASTERN MEXICO
DIAGNOSIS: ASPERGER SYNDROME

MARCO RUNS A FACEBOOK PAGE UNDER
HIS FULL NAME, MARCO ARTURO

(PHOTO: ANTONIO R. FRAUSTO)

"I LIKE KNOWING THAT I CAN DO STUFF EVEN THOUGH IT'S TWICE AS HARD FOR ME (INCLUDING DOING A BUNGY JUMP ON HOLIDAY)."

RACHAEL, AGE 16, FROM AUCKLAND, NEW ZEALAND
DIAGNOSIS: AUTISM, SENSORY SENSITIVITY

Rachael

Gavin

"WHAT I LOVE MOST ABOUT LIFE IS...
MYSELF. I LOVE MYSELF."

GAVIN, AGE 7, FROM LOUISIANA, USA
DIAGNOSIS: ASD, COMPLEX MOTOR STEREOTYPY, OCD

145

Special thanks

From the depths of my heart, I would like to thank the following people:

- *My family, for turning me into the man I am.*

- *My friends, who helped me stay afloat during my darkest times.*

- *The 22nd Nottingham Boys' Brigade, who took the weird kid with zero leadership skills and turned him into a teacher.*

- *Nancy Price, for her tireless efforts and priceless help with the design of this book (and so much more besides).*

- *My lecturers at Nottingham Trent University, for guiding me through my first steps in self-publishing.*

- *The people who bullied me and made me feel incapable over the years. You forced me to prove you wrong, and made me a better person — despite trying to make me worse.*

- *The Autistic Not Weird website & Facebook page participants and followers, whose compassion and character make the community what it is.*

- *And finally, the 150 young people and their parents from 20 different countries, who chose to share their insight with the world.*

A note to young readers across the autism spectrum

None of us are alone. Ever.

If you asked me how many people I've ever known on the autism spectrum, I wouldn't quite know. Hundreds, definitely. I've lost count.

But every one of us sees life differently. Every one of us sees our autism differently too: some are very positive about it, and some are quite negative.

And me? I've been both. At first, I thought my autism was a bad thing. I thought it was something that just got in my way, rather than being a set of strengths that was different to other people's strengths. These days, I know a lot better.

Kids, don' t make the same mistake I made. I spent far too long thinking that difference was 'bad', and normal was 'good'. It took me a while to learn that I'd lose an important part of myself if I tried to be like everybody else.

Yes, during the bad times, autism can feel quite lonely. But take it from me, as someone who has seen the highs and the lows, having a different perspective is often absolutely awesome.

There is so much to love in the world. You've just read the opinions of 150 young people — with brains similar to yours and mine — pointing out some of those wonderful things.

I hope this book has given you more to love about the world, and more to love about being autistic!

All the best to all of you,

Chris

"THE OCCASIONAL, SUDDEN REALISATION THAT YOU'RE A CONSCIOUS LIVING BEING WHO GETS TO EXPERIENCE THE UNIVERSE."

CHRIS, AGE 31, FROM NOTTINGHAM, ENGLAND – DIAGNOSIS: ASPERGER SYNDROME

Chris

"TAILS FROM SONIC THE HEDGEHOG. AND DAYDREAMING. DAYDREAMING ABOUT TAILS."

THE ANSWER I WOULD HAVE GIVEN, AGED 10

About the editor
Chris Bonnello

Chris Bonnello of Nottingham, England, was first assessed for autism in 1989 at the age of four. Despite reporting observations such as "interaction with peers is poor" and "significant delay in expressive language skills, functioning around the 2.5 year level", he did not receive a diagnosis since he was deemed academically capable.

At the age of ten, he was reported by an educational psychologist as having a "slightly odd personality". He grew up believing himself to be the weird kid, until his Asperger Syndrome diagnosis came at the age of 25.

Thankfully, he had a family who focussed on what he was rather than what he wasn't, and a succession of teachers who rooted for him. So after fighting his way through some extremely awkward teenage years (and plenty of therapy as an adult), he earned a degree in Mathematics with Education and a PGCE in Primary Teaching.

Having worked in both primary and special education, he left the profession and launched Autistic Not Weird (AutisticNotWeird.com) in April 2015, to share his insights from a personal and professional perspective.

At time of writing (November 2016) his site has had more than 800,000 pageviews, while his Facebook community (facebook.com/autisticnotweird) has welcomed upwards of 37,000 followers.

Bonnello gives autism talks nationwide (with international aspirations), captains his local Boys' Brigade company, and is halfway through a Masters degree in Creative Writing.

His personality remains slightly odd.

WHAT DO <u>YOU</u> LOVE MOST ABOUT LIFE? WRITE AND DRAW IN THE BOX BELOW AND SAVE IT TO LOOK BACK ON WHEN YOU'RE OLDER!

WHAT WE LOVE MOST ABOUT LIFE

We asked 150 children & teenagers across the autism spectrum:

"What do you love most about life?"

Inside are their answers!

This book offers an uplifting peek into the minds of young people with autism, which is sure to provide other autistic children and teenagers with plenty of reasons to smile.

These insights from kids around the globe were gathered by Chris Bonnello, an autistic former teacher and creator of the website Autistic Not Weird.

ISBN 9781910223833

9000

9 781910 223833